The Ultim Guide fo  ʊ.ɪʊ to Advanced

A short course on learning copywriting that sells, a book/workbook/handbook of web copywriting for business advertising,social media,email

Neil Hoechlin

ISBN-13:
978-1719061131

ISBN-10:
1719061130

Introduction

Copywriting is salesmanship in print, to promote a person, service, position or an idea.

You may introduce this in print, a radio or television promotion, online or in a range of other forms of media. The primary objective of composing a marketing copy is to encourage the audience to respond in a particular way based on the call of action, such as to buy services or products, subscribe, visit a website, sign up for a newsletter, etc.

In the internet marketing world, copywriting is utilized extensively to market, get opt-ins for email lists and to monetize from potential clients. If you genuinely desire to be successful in your online enterprises, you'll have to master the ropes of effective copywriting to guarantee business success. Luckily, good copywriting can be learned.

Copywriting is a discipline, in which you learn through practice and training. If you determine that you're a great writer, the only adjustment you need to make is to learn the right way to write compelling copy that sells well. Copywriting will not be simple to learn. You will have to undertake lots of practice and learning. It is similar to lifting weights for several months or even years until you get solid results! You will develop, but it will be challenging, at least in the beginning.

If you write daily for a particular amount of time, you will develop copywriting abilities to the point where one day you just naturally become great at it. If you focus on copywriting and create material daily, you will eventually evolve into a masterful copywriter, that can print money! You have to understand how to interact with the audience in such a way that persuades them to buy.

There should be a compelling initial connection made. Otherwise, you'll lose the audience's focus.

The knack to transform words into gold is one of the most important skills any entrepreneur needs to succeed.

If you can do this, it does not matter where you are in the world; you can earn money from anywhere, anytime just from your words! How cool is that?

Back in the day, the very best copywriters were also amazing salesmen who were well acquainted with sales techniques to promote anything to anyone. Today, modern-day business owners online are making a killing using copywriting practices in their businesses.

Bear in mind; marketing things online is a tad more difficult than selling things in the real world since you do not have the means to persuade by voice and body language. If you understand precisely the best ways to use the power of copywriting to excite your clients, you 'll be laughing all the way to the bank.

For your development, ensure that you keep training all the time. When you practice and learn every day, you will have consistent growth.

An additional significant component of copywriting mastery is to be abreast of the trends in the market.

Website Product Copywriting

The following are general guidelines you need to be effective in this particular space:

>> A good web design that is not too complicated or overwhelming.

>> A good product

>> A USP or Unique Selling Position

But these are not enough to market, let alone sell products online.

As a copywriter, it is your job is to have your visitor want to stay and respond to your calls to action on the website. Introduce your product the best way possible. Persuade them and make them want to purchase.

Creating a better copy comes from knowing for whom your copy is written. Know your audience, your ideal customer, your buyer's persona. By identifying and understanding your ideal buyer, allows you to anticipate and answer all possible questions or rejections that they may have regarding your product or service.

Leverage on brand storytelling. Good narration helps your reader understand and realize that they have a problem and that your product is what they need to fix that problem. Help your reader imagine themselves being in that story. Make them empathize with your story and relate to it.

You need to have a magnetic headline. It should stand out and be interesting to capture your ideal customer's attention.

Use the 4 U's of marketing copy to guide you in grabbing your prospective customer's attention and get them to take action. That is-be Ultra-specific, be Unique, make sure that your content is Useful, and create a sense of Urgency.

Consider the following when writing a Product Page:

>> Clear product title and price - create a highly descriptive product title. This will help your customer know what it is precisely that you are offering. Be precise and accurate with your pricing information. This is crucial and

one of the deciding factors in their buying decisions. Include any discount or savings that your prospective customer can benefit from their purchase.

>> Concise - Pack only the information that your potential customer needs as clear and succinct as possible. Don't lose customers just because you confused them with useless information that only distracts or does not explain how they can benefit from your product.

>> Bullet points - As much as possible, use bullet points. Most of the time, your reader would only scan your copy looking just for the information that they need. Help them see it by giving the information in a bullet form. Summarize the benefits and features that can be quickly read.

>> Creative - Use your imagination. Be as creative as you can be with your descriptions. The tone of your product description should also match your product and your buyer's persona.

>> Call-To-Action - Convince your page visitor to act now. Be explicit with what you want them to do.

Blog Posts Copywriting

Blogging is a powerful marketing tool. It is a great way to attract potential customers to a website. But no matter how perfect your grammar or interesting your topic is, if no one reads it, then it is just as if it was never there at all. So, it is vital that you make your posts engaging enough to hook your readers and respond to your call-to-action. This is when your copywriter side will come in handy.

Copywriting techniques for a blog post that you can follow:

The 4Us Formula

>> Useful - If your article has no value to the reader, then they will not read it. Make sure that you write a topic that offers something of great value or targets their pain points. Make your reader realize that your copy provides a solution to their problem or answers their question. What is it that your reader is going to gain by reading your text? Always bear in mind the WIIFM (Whats In It For Me) rule, at every moment and with every hoop you make them go through.

>> Unique - While your topic may be similar to several other blogs on the internet, you can still make your posts stand out and be different by adding a little personality, humor, or something that can arouse interest. Surprise them, pique their interest, share a piece of information they never heard of before.

>> Urgency - Create a blog post with a sense of urgency. Your copy should be compelling enough to encourage them to act after reading it. Motivate your reader and convince them that time is of the essence and that they should act now.

>> Ultra-Specific - Avoid using vague topics. Be specific and narrow down your topic as much as possible. It can be a number or a list or a how-to post that is detailed, but specifically to that particular topic alone. This makes your message clear and exciting. Being ultra-specific helps your readers digest the information you are providing. It means that your copy is devoid of useless information or sub-topics that only distracts and diverts their attention.

The AIDA Formula

>> **Attention** - Catchy, and attention-grabbing headlines. Your entire content will be useless if you fail to hook your potential customer from your headline. Don't take for granted the power of a well-crafted headline.

>> **Interest** - Arouse your reader's interest by writing something relatable to their problems or experiences. From opening to the last sentence, you have to keep the momentum going. Keep them wanting for more. Your post should exude with energy that the reader is motivated to read on. Deliver on the promise you made on your headline so they will keep coming back.

>> **Desire** - Make your target audience want to read your article and crave for more. Tap into their emotions and connect with their feelings. Make them want what you are offering or do what you want them to do. Depending on your goal for your post, it should be convincing enough to want what you are pitching. Again, the benefit factor will be all that matters in the end.

>> **Action** - Include a call-to-action on your post. It can be as simple as asking a question that will prompt your readers to comment or participate in a discussion. Engage your reader. You have to be explicit and direct with your request that will satisfy your end goal.

Landing Page Copywriting

The Landing Page

It is a stand-alone web page created specifically for marketing and sales intentions. When your prospective customer clicks on your ad or link, this where you will send them. Typically to generate leads by collecting their names and email, or get the sales right then and there! It should be simple and clutter-free. There are limited navigation buttons or links, which is what makes it different from a basic home page. A website can have many different versions of a sales letter.

Landing pages usually use a lead bait to capture your visitor's information such as a free e-book they give away in exchange for the email.

Why a Landing Page?

The landing page has a single purpose and objective. Convert your visitor into a lead, or make the sale, or any other call to action. They tend to convert more than a homepage because they target a specific audience.

A Homepage is generic and cluttered with links and unnecessary information that your targeted audience won't need. Sending them to your home page will only confuse and disappoint your potential lead because it does not contain the information they need to complete your **Call-To-Action.**

What Makes a Good Landing Page?

Limited Navigation

A good landing page should have limited to no navigation at all. They should be kept to just one page and don't make them exit and enter another page. This will only distract and negatively impacts the visitor's experience. The only time that you will lead your visitor to another page or link is when you are taking them to your CTA.

Meet their Expectations

Meet your visitor's expectation by delivering on what you promised in your ad. The copy on your landing page should match what you promised in your ad. That is what they came for in the first place. And make sure that it is something of value to them.

Encourage Sharing

Encourage your visitors to share your page with a similar audience. This will enhance your reach and organic traffic.

Be Clear and Concise

Be brief and as concise as possible. Do not flood your page with vague and unnecessary information. Your instructions should be clear as well. It will not help your prospect see the value of your offer if you are making them guess on the next steps to take. Worse, they might ultimately abandon your landing page.

Test Variations

Don't be content with just one version. Try using variations on your text to test which landing page copy will convert the most and serve your purpose and goal.

One Goal

Your landing page should only have one goal. Including one too many call-to-actions on your landing page will rob each other's conversion. It is better to create another landing page for your other conversion goal.

The Headline

As in every copy, the headline is your first shot at capturing your prospective customer. Make it as persuasive as possible. Your headline should be compelling enough to get your reader hooked and stay for more. It should engage your readers, arouse their curiosity, entice them to want what you are offering, and motivate them to take action. You should also be clear on your message.

Call-to-Action Copy

Create a strong CTA. Instead of saying "Try it," you instead can say "Download Now for Free."

Convert more by making a Call-to-Action copy that reinforces the benefits. So, if you are offering a How-To Guide e-book on Digital Marketing, for example, instead of saying "Click Here to Download," you could instead state "Show Me How to Be an Effective Marketer."

Readability

Pay attention to the readability of your copy. Consider the line length. The spacing between each line should be the right size so as not to make your copy look compressed or squeezed, or text is too large that they already strain the eyes of the reader. The density of each paragraph should also keep a maximum of four sentences, or you risk scaring away your readers with large blocks of text.

Comprehension

Make your copy easy to understand. Do not use jargons or complicated words. Avoid being ambiguous, but instead be clear and descriptive. So instead of saying your product is "awesome," you could say that it is "fast acting" or "waterproof up to 200 meters"

Proofread

Always check for grammatical or spelling errors as this will hurt your credibility and authority. By creating an error-free and a well-written landing page copy, you tell your visitors that you adhere to high standards and commitment to take care of your customer's information.

Testimonials

Whenever it's available and relevant, incorporate reviews, testimonials, or certifications. This helps in your prospect's decision making and builds trust and confidence.

Bullet Points

A great way to enumerate the benefits is to use bullet points. This helps in keeping your reader engaged and wanting to read more.

Visuals

Include good visuals or images that are relevant to your copy. They help attract readers and improves the overall appeal of your landing page.

The Form

The number of fields in your landing page form should be relevant to the stage of your buyer's journey. For example, a lead capture form should only ask for the name and email address. Don't ask for too much, too soon.

Email Marketing

Email marketing is a form of direct marketing that uses electronic mail for potential customer acquisition, to nurture relationships with customers, build brand or customer loyalty. Since the dawn of electronic mail, email marketing has been an invaluable tool for any business.

Why Email Marketing?

>> Design Flexibility - Depending on your branding and purpose, you can customize every marketing e-mail, including text and other visuals that will help better communicate with your prospects.

>> Measurability - Today's analytics enables you to track how every campaign is doing and which is working and which isn't or needs upgrading.

>> Fast, Time Saving, and Cost-Effective - Email is relatively cheap and easy to set-up compared to other marketing channels. There is no printing cost associated with an email campaign. Unlike direct mail marketing, email marketing allows you to reach your target audience in an instant, think real-time.

>> Targeted Marketing - email marketing will enable you to reach highly targeted and segmented audience. This augurs well as you are more likely to have a higher conversion rate.

>> Less Intrusive - the Potential customer can choose the time and day when they will read your email. As opposed to telemarketing, it is non-intrusive, thus does not affect relationship building.

>> Automation - With automation, you can plan and schedule your email marketing campaign. You can also send email campaigns, according to the triggers set off by your prospects actions on your website, e-commerce site, or previous emails.

Crafting an Effective Email Marketing Copy

>> Killer Subject Line and Preview Text- The best place to start is to write a compelling and eye-catching subject line. The preview is often the first line of your email that is shown by an email software along with your subject line. Think of them as your Headline and Sub-headline. They will either result in your prospect opening, deleting, or considering your email as spam. So make sure that you write a catchy and clear subject line. It should convey the message and compel them to open and read on.

>> Deliver on Your Promise - Align the body of your copy with your subject line. What they will read should be what you had them expect. It should be relevant and answers all possible questions that they may have regarding your product or service.

>> Benefits over Features - Your goal is to convince your reader to act on your email. But they will not even consider clicking that "Buy Now" button unless you have assured them that it will be worth their money and time. Stress on what they will gain from taking advantage of your offer. You can use bullets to make your copy easier to scan and read. Again, its always WIIFM (what's in it for me).

>> Be Brief and Concise - Don't overwhelm your prospective customer with too much information that may not even be relevant. Most of the time, your reader will only scan through your copy and look for keywords that will answer their questions or solve their problem. Keep it direct and on-point.

>> Call-to-Action - Remember that your call-to-action also needs a good copy. Use action verbs. Convince them to act, be explicit with what you want them to do. Consider also the design, size, color of your CTA button and text.

>> Avoid All Caps - Don't make your copy sound aggressive, rude, and arrogant. Avoid using all caps and exclamation as much as possible. Use it only when you need to stress a point. All-caps-text is equivalent to shouting, and nobody wants to be yelled at, right?

>> Split Test - Create and Test each copy to see which performs better.

>> Get Inspiration - There is nothing wrong with emulating past campaigns that resulted in high conversion rate. Utilize swipe files and draw inspiration from them.

>> Psychology Strategy - Tap into their emotions. Use it to trigger a response.

>> Scarcity and Urgency - Nobody wants to miss out on things they will significantly benefit from.

>> Personalize - Email marketing is like writing a personal letter. You are talking to your prospective customer. It is then imperative that you make your reader feel that you are directly talking to them. It adds that special connection and foster engagement.

>> Visuals - Your choice of color, text size, and images all contribute to the overall feel of your copy.

>> Social Proof - Let people who are relatable to your prospective customer, do the talking for you through testimonials and social proof.

Sales Letter

A sales letter is a marketing tool that is intended to persuade prospective customers to purchase a product or service. Through the sales letter, you speak to your potential customer one-on-one. You start with a compelling hook, then highlight the facts, then end with a strong intent to have your reader act and respond positively to your proposition.

The first and arguably the most critical component of a good sales letter is the headline. If you do not grab your target audience's interest rapidly, you will have squandered your time in writing the rest of the copy. What's the point, if they're not going to read the rest anyway?

The 2nd major part of a sales letter is the deal or actual package. This part is the core of it all. You should be explicit with hitting and meeting what the potential customer wants. It needs to be something that they need in their life! It is something that will add value to their life, or solve a particular problem.

The last component of a sales letter is the postscript. This is the second most, checked area of a sales letter after the headline. When you are writing this, aim to offer added encouragement to encourage your prospective customers to get the deal you're suggesting.

You do not merely sit down and make up a sales letter randomly. Instead, you need to tick some boxes in their heads.

This calls for writing the headline (and sub-headlines); creating the bullets (think of them as mini-headlines and sub-headlines, encapsulating specific selling points and concepts); the offer, then the postscript and layering in a bunch of other psychological triggers--cram as many as you can! Therefore, it's crucial that you recognize exactly what your intended outcomes or psychological and emotional effects are before starting.

Sales Page Copywriting

At this stage, you should be able to create a buyer's journey experience pleasant and convincing enough to trust you with his money and purchase your product or service.

You may know your product very well. You may be confident that your product is the solution to their problem. You know that they will derive benefit from your offer.

Your prospect has landed on your sales page, but he has not yet bought. Not yet.

It is your job then to continue the momentum and keep pressing to captivate your prospective customer and make that sale. This is your last opportunity to close that sale. So how do you do it?

>> Nail the Headline - Make it attractive. Promise them an excellent result; they can't resist not wanting it. Make it something persuasive enough that they will want to read what's next. Getting to that part where you can write great headlines needs practice. The more you practice, the better you get at it. Remember to study from the masters! Start building your swipe file!

>> Your Opening Paragraph - Be more detailed here. Keep your prospect captivated and drawn to your copy. Tease them some more.

>> Tell a Story - This is where you need to be more creative. In that, you need to present an ideal scenario that your prospect will find relatable. Use their pain points, explain what causes them to experience such discomfort, explain how your product can cure the cause of the problem, and tell what will happen and how it will benefit them.

>> Understand Your Customer - Understanding well your ideal customers, allows you to create a copy that speaks to them. Their needs, problems, fears and frustrations. It would let you connect to their feelings and be in their shoes. When your prospects feel that you know them, it will be easier for them to trust and hear what you have to say.

>> Show Proof - Include testimonials from past satisfied customers. Case studies that will prove your point and back your claims.

>> Your Offer – Give them an offer they can't resist. Something that is so tempting they cannot just let it pass. Highlight how they will benefit in return. Are you offering discounts? Are you throwing in extras like free shipping? Is your price way cheaper than your competitors? Show them price

comparisons that will demonstrate the difference. Be creative and compelling.

>> Remove Any Objections and Offer Your Guarantee - Think of all possible objections or questions that they may have in mind regarding your product or service. Answer them, address all their concerns. Remove all possible hesitations. Then offer your guarantee that may seal the deal.

>> Scarcity- Show true scarcity. Providing limited time or inventory creates a sense of urgency. This adds as a deciding factor as well.

>> Power Words - There is no denying the impressive power the choice of words could have in the minds of potential customers. The use of power words https://copywritematters.com/copywriter-words-that-sell/ to highlight newness, exclusivity, urgency, savings, pain, etc. Words that your prospect can relate to. Words that get them excited about your product, or feel the urgency to purchase immediately.

>> Call to Action - choose only one call to action. Don't confuse your prospects by asking them to do more than one response. Don't ask them to subscribe and buy at the same time. So choose just one goal and one specific call to action. Stick to that. Make it prominent and stand out.

>> Make it easy to read - You may be required to write a long copy. That is ok. But make your copy easy to understand. Create bullet points; create several paragraphs with a few sentences. Add video or infographics to help your prospects visualize your message.

>> Thorough and Clear - Lastly, be consistently clear and rigorous. Be as comprehensive as possible. Cover all areas of concern, all of the benefits your product provides, all features that make your product stand out from the

rest of your competition. Be as concise, clear, and thorough at the same time. Help your customers make an informed decision.

Keep It Laid-Back

Seem like a friendly person who is additionally an authority, and not just an annoying and pushy salesman. The latter will cause people to dislike you and might start treating you as a threat, who just wants to sell to them!

For many, that zombie state of procrastination ought to be blasted out in the sales-letter!

You may get them to acknowledge that, sure, what you got there, sure sounds like a great deal—but they're not taking action to take the plunge and seal the deal!

Think about this from the prospect's point of view. It can hurt him to squander money on something that won't help him in any way.

Also, if a friend called you out of the blue, how would you talk to him? Now think about how much better it would be if you were talking to a prospect like a good friend? A friend is more likely to trust and take you up on your offer, right?

With our mates, we are more agreeable, a lot more trusting, minimal emotional guards are up, a lot more generous and more caring, etc.

I would also strongly advise you do a little split testing of the elements you put in your letter.

Eliminate things that do not work and replicate or increase what does work. Tweak constantly! And you'll know what to fix by split-testing, or even multivariable testing the elements in the sales copy.

Valuing your customers and your product and services show through in a hundred subtle ways

Does this enthusiasm, this reliability, this compassion shine through in all your marketing and advertising products too? Does it beam through on your website and ales brochures?

When you talk with customers, your genuineness, as well as enthusiasm, is revealed not just in what you say, but in your body language, the tone of your voice, the glimmer in your eye as well as energy and vibe.

Persuading written stuff is not easy to do, because people can't observe powerful, subtle messages and nuances.

Here are some things you could do with your written products to demonstrate you care:

>> Know what keeps your prospect up at night and be sure your sales letter addresses those worries in a compelling and personalized way.

>> Appreciate their difficulties as well as other concerns.

>> When you are genuinely concerned about your client's well-being, it will shine through in your writing.

>> Write like how you talk.

>> Be conversational, also, write at a 5th-grade comprehension level.

>> No big words or words that you have to clarify the meaning, unless if you believe it to be necessary to talk highbrow and technical.

>> Give examples of people, you've worked with as well as how you've helped them.

>> Be yourself and let your character (or at least the persona) show using your writing. Find your voice!

Understanding Your Prospects

First, you should do your research. You should understand all there is to understand what makes him tick. Create a mental image of your prospect. What age is he/she? How rich or poor? What does he drive? What's his ethnicity? Write the sales letter for that ONE PERSON ONLY! That person is the avatar or representation of all your prospects! What causes him pain? Find that wound, stick a knife into it, twist it, THEN offer your solution. If you can't make them connect with their grief? Your medicine or solutions, won't appear as valuable.

You need to concentrate on REALLY narrowing down who you are writing the sales letter for, and what particular pains you are trying to fix.

Great copywriting is a lot more than just merely describing the qualities and perks of the service or product you are attempting to sell. If you are selling to thousands of chiropractors for example? As mentioned, envision what that idea would look like if personified into a single person and imagine you are talking with that person in a casual, relaxed environment, such as at a bar or party somewhere. What would you say and how would you say it?

The Ideal Customer

They are the target of your copy so it is crucial that you know your audience well, understand their fears, pains, happiness and other emotional buttons. This is the only way that you can create a copy that can stimulate their emotions and cause them to take the action that you want.

Knowing your ideal customer is about getting inside their skin and understanding their challenges, how they think and what they feel. Necessary information like age, gender, education level, income level, and the location is essential to know, to form a general profile. Depending on the product or service that you offer; you can expand the demographics to create the profile of your ideal customer. A great way to learn and gain more insight into your perfect customer is by conducting a survey. There are a lot of survey tools, free and paid alike, that you can use to serve this purpose. It allows you to research, reach more audience, and get their responses fast and efficiently.

Their Pains and Struggles

Your ideal customer's pain points are specific problems they are currently struggling with and would need help.

What frustrates your ideal customer? What do they struggle with that your product or service can address or solve? This is crucial and an integral part of your research. Knowing what they struggle with and how you can remedy those problems. It will help you connect with your potential customers. Sometimes, your prospective customers are not even aware that they have a problem. Which is the reason, you need to dig deeper into your research to form an in-depth profile. It will then be your job to help them realize this problem and convince them that you have the solution.

Second, you have to know just ways to structure your letter.

The Sales Letter Structure

There is an order to follow when you provide the details and make your offer Identify the most suitable structure for composing a robust copywriting piece

Understanding your prospect is very important if you want to develop copy that sells. Anytime you do not understand your customer, you will not understand the concerns they have, and thus the perfect solutions that hit the right spot!

When you do understand your prospect, you'll know how to hit their hot switches and which feelings to trigger and which benefits to focus on. You can even present a personal story that they can connect with strongly.

The most effective educational marketing products do three things:

1. Make your potential clients understand their issues and how it's painfully affecting their lives. Dimensionalize and make these problems real in their mind!

2. Program them just how your service/product offers a practical way to get what they WANT.

3. Offer them a way to improve their situation right now.

Headline Essentials

The headline is the essential part of any copy.

If your headlines fail to get the focus of your readers, it will not say how great your offer will be. You have 5 seconds to make an impact on your visitors before moving on, so make it count. The headline needs to be eye-catching and bolded to get your audience's attention, and stop them in their tracks!

Crafting a great headline is imperative in every sales copy. Your goal is to make your reader, read your first sentence. If you fail to accomplish this, then the rest already failed. That is why the attention-grabbing headline is critical and should be carefully thought out.

Think of it this way; your headline is your first chance to make a good impression. It should be compelling enough to have your reader glued to your copy and continue reading.

Your headline provides the gist of what benefit you offer and should arouse their curiosity enough to dig further down on what you are saying.

Types of Headlines

There many ways you can write your compelling headline. Depending on your target audience and purpose, each class has its unique way of attracting customers and compel them to take action, if used correctly. Here are some examples to model on your headline.

>> Direct Headlines - Is straight to the point. No frills, no thrills type thing. You tell directly to your readers what it is your selling proposition. Examples like "Pink Baby Dresses - 25% Off", "Guide to Home Buying Free E-book."

>> News Headlines - As the title suggests, your headline speaks to announce or introduce a new product or improvements. "Introducing Newest Version of XXX App"

>> How-To Headline - A sure fire way of enticing potential customers who seek information or advice on how to solve their pain points relevant to the product or service that you are offering. Such as, "How to Write a Sale Copy That Sells."

>> Question Headline - A headline that asks the question that potential readers might relate to, empathize, or just plain curious to get to know the

answer. An example, could be something like, "Do you make these mistakes in your Sales Ads?"

>> Command Headline - A headline that hinges on a strong action verb that encourages your prospect to act on your offer that will benefit them like, "Download Your Free Copywriting Guide E-book Today."

>> Reason-Why Headline - Gives your prospects reason to read your whole sales copy. It is specific in that you provide some features, benefits, or tips that your reader will get. An example would be, "10 Ways to Write a Great Copy That Sells".

>> Testimonial Headline - This where you leverage on the actual testimonials of your customers. It is compelling in that you have your customer speaking on your behalf and selling for you by declaring or claiming to have benefited from your product or service. Or even providing proof of how and what pain points your product has solved for them. Imagine a happy customer speaking for you in this way, "Reed's 'Complete E-Commerce Guide E-book' Helped Me Make $20K in Sales."

>> Benefit Headline - You state the benefits and squeeze them in a single but compelling sentence. You need to make sure that you have done your research enough to know your market that your headline targets directly their pain points and what solution you offer.

It may read something like, "Fairer Skin in Five Days."

Bullets

Bullets are a powerful way of highlighting your features and benefits without drowning your reader with information and potentially discouraging them from further reading your sales letter. You focus your reader's attention by enumerating the info you want to present to your potential customers with the help of bullet points. But you have to be succinct and direct to the point. Another trick is to mention the benefit first, then the feature.

For example:

>> Non-stick Fast Heating Iron plate cuts down ironing time in half

>> Free shipping on your first 50 units and save $25 becomes, Cut down your ironing time in half with Nonstick Fast Heating Iron Plate.

>> Save $25 on shipping when you order your first 50 units

Bullet points can be compelling when used correctly. They are not intimidating and reader-friendly. It allows you to summarize your selling points without the need for smooth transitioning from one to another.

Subheadings/Sub-Headline

While the headline is the first information that your potential customer reads, the subheading provides your reader a more in-depth explanation of your purpose and selling point.

It is just as important as your heading. This needs to be engaging enough to encourage your potential customer to stick around for more. Avoid using weak and vague statements, but instead be specific and convincing.

Why does a Sub-Headline Matter?

Your sub-headline acts as the extension of the heading. After grabbing your reader's attention with the headline, your sub-heading should be able to keep the momentum, and your reader intrigued enough to read more of your copy. To make your subheading more effective, it has to be just the right length. It should also contain just the appropriate amount of information and persuasion. So don't overdo it. You still have the rest of your sales letter to do that.

Some Common Ways to Create an Engaging Subheading

>> Make a claim or a promise. As long as you're confident with your product or service and you know that it is what your ideal customer wants. It is essential as well that you support it further with the rest of your sales copy

>> Loaded questions. Tease them with an intriguing question. Have your reader think or react, and get them to read for more information.

>> Help them imagine themselves standing out from the crowd. Nothing beats the feeling of being somebody unique or outstanding. You are tapping on this emotional need.

>> Highlight the specific problem you are solving by your product or service.

>> Unique Offer. Highlight why your offer stands out from the rest of the competition.

>> Focus on the Benefits. Draw your customer deeper into your sales letter by highlighting what they can benefit from your product or service.

>> Debunk Myths or Misconceptions. A more creative way of arousing your reader's curiosity that you can later leverage upon to draw attention to what your product can offer.

>> Reveal. Tell your prospects what it is they are getting in exchange.

The sub-headline will enhance the message of the headline. Jot down the advantages of your product and the advantages for your target group, not yourself.

Make them into a collection of various heading alternatives or possibilities.

>> Why lazy ----- be successful in ----- and good guys fail.

>> Why lazy males are successful in internet marketing and good guys stop working.

>> Who else wants to ----- with/in -----.

>> What everybody ought to learn about -----.

>> For individuals who wish to ----- but can't get started.

>> These are probably the best kept ----- secrets worldwide.

>> The quickest method I know-----.

>> The incredible art of -----.

You should also gain tremendous value from examining other sales letters or Swipe files. There's no other secret to master this craft, but to study many proven sales letters!

USP versus ESP

USP or Unique Selling Proposition

Positioning your product or service as the best choice in the market for a specific, well-targeted aspect of a niche is what makes you unique, and much more noticeable in the market.

Among the most harmful mistakes companies make is not standing out enough and not positioning themselves as the best in a particular niche. You can't be everything to everyone, you need to separate a vast industry to sub-niches, and your products and services are the BEST offering one-of-a-kind products and services. Easier said than done, I know, but have that goal when creating your packages.

Having a USP will considerably enhance the positioning and marketability of your products.

Ask yourself; you're operating in which particular niche?

What words can you make use of to arouse strong feelings and perhaps drama in your specific niche?

What sort of words/stories/situations that people in your particular niche can they identify?

Your value proposition or unique selling proposition is a statement that explains how your solutions work, what benefits your customers are bound to get when they purchase your product, why and how different you are from your competitors. What makes you unique!

It should be prominent on your copy. Remember, you need to stand out and get noticed. So take your unique selling proposition or value proposition seriously.

Crafting a Value Proposition

>> Your unique value proposition should be relevant to your prospect's pain points. That means knowing your prospective customer. Understanding them would allow you to think as they do. Feeling as they will let you say the right words that will connect with them and clinch that deal. When you are creating a value proposition, you can't just guess and hope you hit the mark. Or risk not only losing their interest in your product or service but their trust as well.

>> Complete your story. It is not enough that you have described efficiently what your product has (features) and that you have communicated what's in

it for them (benefit). But have them imagine what is going to be the result for them (emotional benefit).

If you are offering a photo app, for example, its main features could be "User-friendly interface, Intelligent, quick touch-up, just press and go". Then its immediate benefit could be, "Stunning, Great Looking, and Instagram Worthy photos on the fly." Then you can fire them up with, "For photos that get more likes, more shares. Get ready to be famous".

>> Show you are better. You may have lots of competition in your niche. Your product may be similar to others in the market. But you can still show them that it is unique by highlighting on what makes your product or service better than your competitors.

You don't have to be better in all aspects. You can be better in one specific aspect alone, that aspect of improvement that your readers are looking for and wanting to have. Think about that one thing that screams; you are "One-of-a-kind."

>> Be as targeted as you can. Don't try to sell your proposition to everyone. Know your targeted market and concentrate on them alone. Having that in mind will help you pick the word that will speak to them and show them what they need and want to scc.

>> Show proof. Sometimes, your claims are not enough. Make your story believable with testimonials or case study results that speaks in your products' favor. Show them you are genuine.

>> Be understandable. Speak to your prospective customers in a language that they can understand. Speak to them in terms that will get your message across effectively. Don't make them wonder what you meant. Be clear and

easy to be understood. Again, this comes from understanding your ideal customer as well.

>>Add a little of something. Depending on your product or service that you offer, you can also throw in one or two complimentary add-ons. Such as free shipping, installation, free upgrade, or money back guarantee.

Establishing Your Areas of Difference

Why are you different and a lot better than other people? Now is the correct time for you to boast! Apprise them of things you have accomplished, what you have done for other people and how they too can get the same outcomes.

" This college dropout went from a $ delivering pizza to retiring at age 30 with x, xxx, xxx dollars.

He's coached numerous individuals just like you to generate serious dough on the Internet."

We have something called Emotional Selling Point - that is the power to tap into the emotions of your customers so that you can make them carry out your call to actions.

Here's an example of a selling point, that is psychological in nature.

I know what it's like to be a struggling online marketer. Sometimes, I could only afford a sandwich for the day because I wasn't generating income from my online businesses...

This conventional example relates the struggle faced by the marketer to the person reading the sales copy, who is most likely dealing with the same problems that he later on overcame.

Story Driven Copywriting

A story driven copy is generally a great persuader. You will find three components, which can be essential in every story.

1 - The Challenge - that which you have to do.

2 - The Struggle - The trials and adversities you experienced while carrying it out.

3 - The Resolution - How you succeeded.

It's crucial you are using stories that are believable. Your readers must see you as a genuine human being who experienced and solved the problem. Make sure you do not rehash stories told a thousand times.

Help The Reader Picture and Feel

It isn't adequate to just make offers and claims on your copy; you will have to assist the reader picture it in their minds.

You are going to need to guide them to see and feel it, and a copywriter who is good at his job can have you imagining it too. It isn't that logical thinking is terrible, it's just that logic is chums with skepticism, and quickly you will see a hundred reasons why you should not believe a word.

Just think of the marketing and advertising that you last saw about cars. Heaps of high-end, hot scantily clothed girls with the best faces and bodies and so on. Why was that necessary? Guide your reader to picture good things! Make him lust after it! The awesomeness of the service or product. Do not just let them understand this logically.

Great copy results in the promise of beautiful things-- of what your product or service can do in reality for them. That your reader can visualize and connect with it in their life circumstances.

Call to Action (CTA)

The call to action might be one of the top vital aspects of any piece of copy. What you initially need to do is identify what is the most desired results you wish for your customers/prospects.

Establish the problems and how your prospects need some help. These might include, their wants, needs, and desires.

Present the merit and benefits your prospects and clients will get from you if they avail of your service or product.

Spell it out in their mind exactly what they will get if they avail. Make sure that these benefits are highly specific on what your target audience needs or desires.

Make sure that your marketing message is sincere which will speak volumes about what your business is indeed about.

Catch the attention of your prospects and customers with a statement that gives a bright idea of what you're about, and who is your target audience.

Whether you are targeting current industry pros or seasoned veterans, you need to start strong with something that honestly speaks to them, and why they should listen to you. That you indeed know what you're saying! You have the knowledge, know-how, and success to back it up!

Describe your product or service in depth, which will include its functions and their highlights, which again targets your audience's deepest desires and needs.

Include a call to action or CTA in your marketing message and be highly specific about this. You should be direct in telling your potential customers, what you need them to do. Do you want them to sign up for a newsletter? Call your agents? Buy it now? Be specific and strong! Include the WHY's, on why they must do it, including the benefits and the dire consequences if they don't take action today. The general scarcity and price countdown trick before the price goes up, are often employed for this purpose.

Provide useful info for visitors that highlights that taking action is needed immediately.

You must be able to get a prospect to act on it and he needs to relate strongly to a benefit since they are risking their resources and their time.

Clients do not appreciate having their time squandered. If a company is selling a product or service, a universal appeal that will encourage them to respond to a call to action on the spot would be to provide something at a discounted rate or perhaps free of charge. Free trial offers, fully functional software that works for 30 days only, free consultation, etc. are examples of that idea.

They will always ask in the back of their minds, "what's it in for me?".

When a prospect has determined the possibility of getting beneficial results, the positioning, color, and number of repetition or frequency of the call to action are vitally important to hammer the point across.

A right call to action would be - "If you like this article or have ideas, please press like or comment below!"

To offer another example, if you want the prospects to make a purchase, you might ask them to snap it up before supplies run out!

Adding scarcity elements or time sensitivity to the call to action often result in better conversions, so never forget to include it in whatever you are doing.

Finally, you should keep in mind that the success rate of the call to action is not entirely due only to the words used, but the approach in how you developed the different parts of your sales letter such as USPs, dealing with objections, showing the benefits and the general package!

It is vital to use a mix of compelling sales points with active mental triggers. Many who create a sales page miss some of those elements. Now, when they neglect to spray in psychological triggers, nobody will feel compelled to continue reading, since the advantages have an average or low perceived value.

When a visitor does not feel compelled enough to take out his/her wallet at that minute, you have to put out multiple calls to action - another kind of mental trigger.

Managing Objections

Handling objections is an essential skill in copywriting as you can probably already tell. Prospects have questions surface in their mind in an attempt to protect themselves from losing money. This is natural and to be expected, and if you know ways to manage these objections effectively in your copy, you'll start gaining huge rewards.

These doubts are called objections in face-to-face sales. In written sales copy, you need to attend to this with logical, legitimate proof that your product can, in truth, do everything you claimed.

You can put yourself in the prospect's place or point of view, and approach the matter with the same goals and trepidations.

The prospect will not trust you, till he's sure that you appreciate his situation. If you pay attention to the objection and agree, you can be in a position to recommend another solution that offers whatever he has now, plus an advantage that will help him at the same time, which apparently will be valuable to you too.

Here are a few frequently used strategies for handling objections:

Reviews

Social proof is something everybody looks for when they want to get a product. The more reputable the recommendation seems, the more prospects consider the merchandise is of high quality.

You may obtain them from customers that loved your service or product. The formula for an effective review:

>> What was it like, before acquiring the items?

>> The results after trying the items?

>> Put the name, city and URL address. This shows they are from the actual individuals.

The Guarantee

Any credible item should offer a guarantee. Just making use of the word "guarantee" is not enough. Tell them exactly what will occur if they are not happy. Whenever you remove the most prominent obstruction of being cheated on or wasting money, you increase your conversion rates.

FAQS

Creating a frequently asked questions section may assist substantially in getting rid of some objections that may appear. Here you can address all the common mistaken beliefs that might sprout up, such as how to use the product, for whom is the product suitable for and price concerns.

Postscripts (P.S)

P.S or Postscripts have now been utilized thoroughly in sales letters to improve conversions. This is the small summary of what they'll be getting when they choose to buy the item.

Great Reasons Why You Should Buy

This section provides your readers a few factors, to assist them to justify their purchase and significantly raise your revenues.

Subheadings

Readers have tired eyes. The Internet keeps on cranking out more of these sales letters every day. So make your copy appealing. Slice your copy up by making use of sub-headings and bullet points.

Don't make people read too much to get the crucial points. To generate a good impression in your client's mind, the best alternative is to exhibit something, which represents the quality of your product and services.

By this approach, customers can indeed get the value of your product or services. It is important to show the need for your item.

Ad Errors

Test your ads BEFORE it heads out. Find and correct every error!

>> Do the links work?

>> What about the telephone number?

>> What does the voicemail recording say.

Price

Don't shy away from publishing the price. But perhaps it would be best to make a full presentation, rather than just blasting them with the price right away.

Don't aggravate readers and make them search unnecessarily.

Order Options

Buyers want choices. Let them have some.

Set up various ordering systems such as email links, toll-free numbers, fax numbers, postal and online options, payment through Paypal, credit card and so on

Legibility

Can it be easily read by the target audience?

Elderly audiences frequently need bigger typeface sizes than more youthful target audiences. The color schemes also, in general, will differ depending on the target market.

More information

Offer more details. Maybe offer free ebooks, reports and such.

Free-items

People desire free samples, trials; bonus offers or anything before they spend cash!

Copywriting Mistakes To Avoid

Everyone makes errors in their marketing career. This section aims to help you lessen these.

Trying to sell before first giving value

Before you blast your customers with deals, you must continually give free value and develop a relationship that is real, not parasitic.

Sounding too formal

Let's face it; when your pitch sounds too formal, you'll come off as a sales robot and insincere also. Make it so that they could identify with you, and as a result, you'll be closing those sales.

Wasting your reader's time

To write excellent copy, you need to only be including things which add to the desire to purchase (or whatever preferred CTA). Your reader's attention is precious, so if you manage to capture their attention, make it count.
Do not bore these folks with petty stuff. Simply put, if you prevent these errors and diligently practice copywriting strategies, you'll get better in no time at all and crank out more sales.

Make a claim without proof

Any moron can claim to be the smartest guy in the world. Whoever can prove it, however, will be acknowledged as legit. That is the same rule with your copy too.

You have to show proof when you tell people how something is supposedly fantastic.

Back up your claims with practical reasoning, data, reviews and other supporting proof.

Attempting to sell to everyone

If you try to sell to everyone, you're never going to sell to anyone. The higher the specificity, the better it will affect the targeted consumer.

Do not begin at the start

The hardest part of a sales letter to compose is the headline plus the opening paragraphs. Start with some stuff that is simple and easy. If you do get concepts for the headline, take note of them and after that return to whatever you're doing.

Drafting a complete page from blank is difficult for anybody, especially for someone who does not believe in themselves as a writer or a copywriter.

Humor doesn't translate

Many copywriters have a fantastic grasp of humor that works well for them. There are cultures, where humor will not translate well. Clearly, you will find exceptions.

Stop playing with words. While humor can fit still in, an essential point you would wish to prevent in international copywriting is a play on words.

Although we like to have fun with words, again, not everything equates well. Start thinking of an expression that is widely known let's say 'dead in the water.' Incorporate this into your copy.

Humor or humor?

You probably consider US English as standard English, if you're a US copywriter. UK copywriters feel the same about 'English' English.

Be flexible

Stuff is different overseas - it is, after all, another country.

Many US and UK ad agencies have extensive departments entirely devoted to proofing and editing.

Unless you're sure your copy will just be used in a particular place? Make your copy flexible and easily customizable, that the feel and essence of the copy remain the same even when translated to other English speaking nations.

Leave Out Needless Words

Everyone usually has less patience when they're checking stuff out online, so you're well advised to help keep it as brief as you possibly can.

* Use in between 14 and 16 words in each sentence.

* Avoid using jargon unless the majority of your readers know very well what they mean.

* Use language that is not too complicated.

* Use one thought or idea per paragraph.

Discuss Your Prospects' Issues

Countless writers and marketers make the mistake of speaking about themselves in a way the potential customers will find fascinating. The reality is, people are just thinking about your product or services for their own use, not yours. How it will benefit them.

If you're able to grab their attention right away and show that you understand why they need your product or service? You have an outstanding chance of transforming them into customers.

Swipe Files

This section handles swipe files-- you could quickly utilize and copy and paste into the sales copy.

Should you ever want to find out more about preparing great copy, check out l the stuff of copywriting greats like John Carlton, Dan Kennedy, Bencivenga, Jay Abraham, etc.

Dan Kennedy is an example of the world's foremost specialists in direct selling and reading through his handbook provides you with some insights into how to develop effective copy.

The Better Letter Checklist:

>> Does the audience identify with you in the first few lines of the letter?

>> Does your reader immediately know that this conversation is written only for him? When writing copy, imagine you are writing it for one person alone

>> Is urgency established? Does the reader feel he should take action right away or else?

>> Does the letter begin strong - with a crescendo - and then maintaining urgency and interest like a great novel?

>> Did you address and overcome all potential and hidden objections?

>> Maybe you managed to eliminate jargon, catchphrases, and big, hard-to-understand words? Is the letter now easier to read?

>> Is the message personalized with the recipient's name?

>> Is the message about the reader's issues? Does he know what he can expect if he gets your product?

>> Are action words there - e.g., disappear, devastate, ruin...?

>> Is a sharp hook available to grab attention?

>> Is there a loud call to action?

>>Does the P.S. stand alone? Will your reader get the point, even if he doesn't read the whole letter?

>> "You" and "Your" used more often than "We" and "Our?"

>> Has the features been transformed into meaningful benefits?

>> Is authority established? Does the reader think the writer is a professional? That he know what he's talking about?

>> Does the letter contain testimonials, statistics or endorsements from third-parties?

>> Does the message give more than one primary reason to do something? Does it appeal to a variety of motivations by presenting valid arguments?

Finishing up

The capacity to sell via your words and make bank is undoubtedly possible and learnable in a systematic way. It is also an art and craft that can be honed. Your task as a marketer is to vigilantly practice these methods every day.

The more copy you write, the better you will quickly get, and you'll have the ability to churn out world-class sales copies with ease.

Don't be dissuaded if, for example, the sales copy does not convert well the first time. Keep tweaking your copy and remove anything that does not work and change them with items that do.

The authors, publishers, and distributors of this guide have made every effort to ensure the validity, accuracy, and timely nature of the information presented here However, no guarantee is made, neither direct nor implied, that the information in this guide or the techniques described herein are suitable for or applicable to any given individual person or group of persons, nor that any specific result will be achieved The authors, publishers, and distributors of this guide will be held harmless and without fault in all situations and causes arising from the use of this information by any person, with or without professional medical supervision The information contained in this book is for informational and entertainment purposes only It not intended as a professional advice or a recommendation to act

No part of this book may be reproduced or transmitted in any form whatsoever, electronic, or mechanical, including photocopying, recording, or by any informational storage or retrieval system without express permission from the author

Other books by the author

The Complete Day Trading Education for Beginners: a course book to successfully setup & learn the rules, secrets, techniques, psychology, systems & strategy for stocks, futures, forex, etfs & more

Mastering Business Social Media Marketing Theory & Practice: book covers the fundamental facts & strategies, automation & advanced ideas & tips on corporate social marketing for businesses & beyond

Investing In Stock Market For Beginners: Understanding the basics of how to make money with stocks

Real Ways to Make Money Fast Online from Home for Beginners: quickly make easy money on the internet for kids, teens stay at home moms, freelance writers, college students & more...

The Best Real Estate Book for Beginners: Winning in the game of Real Estate Investments!

Customer Service Care Support Success for Life: Exceptional client services, support & behavior by becoming customer centric & obsessed to improve retention, engagement, experience & lifetime value

Made in the USA
Lexington, KY
29 June 2018